Story of an Indian Girl: Many Lived, I Wrote

Nadakkavu, Kozhikode, Kerala, 673011
www.insightpublica.com
e-mail: insightpublica@gmail.com
Title: **Story of an Indian Girl: Many Lived, I Wrote**
Author: **DR ANAGHA POULOSE**
First Insight Edition: May 2025
Printed and Published by
InsightinPublica Printers & Publishers Pvt. Ltd.
ISBN: 978-93-5517-693-6
₹ 150

Story of an Indian Girl: Many Lived, I Wrote

BY

DR ANAGHA POULOSE

INSIGHT PUBLICA®

CONTENTS

Birth of an Indian Girl: The Unwelcomed Dawn 13

"The Mango Tree Rules:

A Daughter's Life in Don'ts" 18

"Candied Wounds: Trust Torn by

Hands That Shouldn't" 20

Teenage: "From Shadows to Light" 24

Love: The Portrait of Her Heart 27

"Brushstrokes of First Love" 31

The Silent Separation 34

"Chasing Dreams, Defying Fate" 37

College days 40

Forced marriage- chained soul 42

First night –"Crushed body and mind" 44

The Shadowed Silence 46

"The Child That Never Was" 50

"From Pain to Power" 52

Unchained 55

Her Second Life 57

The Woman Who Painted Her Destiny 59

"Meeting Her Love, One Last Time—As a Victorious Woman" 62

Free Bird: Unbound and Undone 65

About the Author

Dr Anagha Poulose is a passionate and introspective young woman from Ernakulam, Kerala, with a deep-rooted love for the arts and literature. She has won numerous accolades in both literature and science, consistently balancing creative expression with academic excellence. Trained in classical dance and experienced in modelling, she brings a multidisciplinary perspective to her work, blending artistic expression with thoughtful reflection. She was also an active clinical researcher and has co-authored several research articles published in international journals, including Annals of the Rheumatic Diseases and The Lancet Rheumatology. She has also worked in clinical research and pharmacovigilance with the global organisation IQVIA. A strong advocate for gender equity and women's empowerment, she integrates her feminist values into all aspects of life. Currently based in the UK, Dr Anagha is pursuing postgraduate studies with a focus on cancer research.

PREFACE

"Some ideas stir the soul,
Steal your sleep, haunt the quiet.
Until at last, with trembling pen,
You set them free through ink on paper."

There are times when certain thoughts, ideas, and observations quietly take root within us and refuse to fade. No matter how much we try to suppress them, the fire they ignite continues to smoulder in the corners of our minds. I cannot precisely recall the moment I decided to write this book—perhaps because it did not begin with the intention of becoming a book at all. Writing has always been a quiet refuge for me. I often documented fleeting emotions, reflections, and poetic lines in my diary—short musings that helped me process the world around me. One evening, after returning home from a long and exhausting working day, I penned four simple lines in my journal. There was something about those lines that lingered; their essence stayed with me like a whisper that refused to leave. Each evening thereafter, as I returned from work, I found solace in the presence of my writing desk. What began as a brief entry slowly unfolded into a meditative process of creation. Day by day, those four lines began to expand—growing, evolving, breathing—until they formed the foundation of a longer poem. I never rushed it; instead, I chose to dwell in silence, patiently waiting for the right words, the right emotions, and the right images to arrive. The journey from thought to expression was sacred. This poem was born in the quiet of the night, flowing from mind to paper under the soft glow of a table lamp, with only the cold breeze as its silent witness.

The experience of womanhood is both a sacred gift and an enduring struggle—a journey marked by resilience, grace, and quiet battles often fought in silence. Throughout my life, I have witnessed numerous girls and women endure discrimination, stereotyping, and systemic injustice. Female foeticide, denial of education, forced marriages, dowry demands, domestic violence, child trafficking, and brutal assaults are widespread issues that continue to afflict Indian society. I have also seen women who lacked the support or strength to challenge these norms, resigning themselves to their suffering as if it were their fate. It is my deepest wish that they find the strength to overcome these challenges, but tragically, only a few can do so.

In this book, I have attempted to narrate the story of a girl who endured prejudice, discrimination, harassment, and countless hardships. Yet, like the mythical phoenix, she rises, not untouched by pain but transformed by it. Her journey is not one of defeat but of quiet triumph. Her journey, from birth, through adversity, to resilience, is not hers alone. It is the story of many women in India and indeed across the globe. Through her, I explore themes of grace, ambition, trauma, love, pain, healing, and strength.

I hope that this poem becomes a source of inspiration for my women readers and encourages my male readers to foster greater empathy, respect, and equality, not special treatment, but a genuine acknowledgment of equal worth to the women around them.

I envision a world where humanity collectively honours the essence of feminism a world where compassion and equity flourish. I wrote this book with deep empathy for the humans, and I bled with sorrow in my heart as I composed some of its most poignant sections.

I sincerely thank my parents for believing in the goodness of my dreams and encouraging me to follow my heart. I am also deeply grateful to all the empathetic souls who have extended their love, support, and encouragement throughout my journey.

I dedicate this work to the countless brave and compassionate women I have met, seen, heard, or read about in my life.

As you turn these pages, you will step into a world shaped by a girl's dreams, her sorrows, her strength, and her courage. It is a story for every girl who dares to dream and for every reader willing to listen with empathy.

Birth of an Indian Girl: The Unwelcomed Dawn

After years of marriage, hopes did bloom,

When pregnancy arrived, they whispered in the room:
"Let it be a boy," they all prayed with grace,
For the house had daughters, filling every space.
Her grandfather's wish, with an earnest plea,
"Let this one be a boy, for all to see."

The weight of tradition, on her shoulders it lay,
To bear an heir, she was meant to obey.
Once deemed barren, her husband now smiled,
A gift, he called her, like a treasure beguiled.
Each day he kissed her, fed her with sweets,
Hoping for a son, as love's heartbeat.

After years of waiting for a child, at last,
Her heart leapt, her joy unsurpassed.

But as the days wore on, and the longing grew,
She felt a weight that no one knew.
What if the child was a girl, not a boy?
Would her family still love her, or destroy?
Would her husband's affection turn cold as ice,
If she bore a daughter, not his dream's device?
Her only desire: a healthy child to hold,
Yet the pressure to bear an heir took its toll.

As days passed, her heart filled with fear,
Each kiss on her forehead felt insincere,
A silent command, a constant refrain:
"You must give me a boy, to ease my pain."

Then came the day, a storm of despair,
As sharp as a thousand needles, tearing the air.
Her family rushed her, as her vision grew dim,
Unconscious, she heard a cry faint and slim.
Her heart soared, the pain disappeared,
She smiled, as a mother's love appeared.
In that moment, the world felt right,
She was a mother, bathed in pure light.
Her pain faded, replaced by bliss,
A child was born, her heart's true kiss.

When her eyes fluttered open, she searched in haste,
For the child she had borne, her heart a quiet space.
A nurse appeared, like an angel from dreams,
Cradling a babe with a soft, gentle gleam.

In a cloth wrapped tight, with a red face so pure,
The moment was perfect, serene and sure.

The nurse placed the baby in her waiting hands,
She held her with care, as love understands.
A smile bloomed wide, and she kissed the soft skin,
In that instant, she knew motherhood within.
Her heart was full, her joy complete,
A bond so deep, it could not be beat.

But then, as if struck by a whisper of thought,
She unwrapped the cloth with trembling hands,
She gazed at the face, and tears filled her eyes,
For her child, she realized, was not the boy's prize.
A girl, her child, a daughter to keep,
And with that, she wept, her emotions so deep.

She kissed the baby again, pressing close to her chest,
Fighting the storm that wouldn't let her rest.
"My child is a girl," she sobbed, heart torn,
A mother of a daughter, from the moment she was born.

Yet worry clouded her love, a fierce, quiet fear,
For the battles her child would face, year after year.
The world was harsh, and what it would see,
Would be a girl, not a boy, as it ought to be.
But despite all her doubts, her love stayed strong,
For in her arms, she knew she belonged.
The nurse, with force, pried the child from her grasp,
Her hands now trembling, as if caught in a clasp.
The nurse smiled, but it was hollow, void of care,
"Your family awaits," she said, cold as the air
Terror gripped her heart, her hands shook in fear,

As the nurse disappeared, her child not near.

Outside, her husband stormed in, full of pride,
The nurse passed the child, his joy amplified
He felt like a hero, a man reborn,
Beaming at his family, as if he'd won
A crown of glory, a king of old,
But what would happen next, was something cold.

His mother snatched the child, her eyes quick to judge,
She glanced at the baby, then gave a slight nudge,
"It’s a girl..."—her voice sharp, like a knife,
That single phrase cut through life.

The joy in the hallway, so quickly erased,
Faces turned dark, as hope was displaced.
His father, without a glance, turned away,
No warmth in his eyes, no love to convey.
Instead of holding the child with pride,
They all saw her as a burden to hide.

The baby was passed back, like an unwanted chore,
And the nurse left with her, to be seen no more.
And so, begins the tale, with struggle and fight,
The story of a middle-class Indian girl, seeking the light.
A life shaped by trials, yet filled with grace,
Where love may grow, and hope finds its place.

"The Mango Tree Rules: A Daughter's Life in Don'ts"

She was a vibrant child, a radiant flame,
Graceful and charming, untouched by blame.
A family drawn to her innocent glow,
A girl's love blossomed, no boy could bestow.

Her grandfather's heart, once heavy, soon melted,
Months of her laughter, his love was cemented.
A princess she became, the house her domain,
Her mother's old worries dissolved in the rain.

Yet her father, a fortress, withheld his affection,
His love masked in orders, in cold recollection.
Obey, he demanded; her spirit suppressed,
Her childhood dreams slowly repressed.

Years flew by, love turned to care too severe,
She climbed a mango tree without any fear.

Her father, enraged, pulled her down with haste,
A beating ensued; her innocence displaced.

"Girls don't climb trees," his harsh voice declared,
A dozen more "girls don't" followed, ensnared.
Girls don't run wild, don't laugh too loud,
Don't question rules, don't stand too proud.
Don't dream of stars, don't chase the sun,
Don't act like you're equal to anyone.

"Sit properly," warned the aunt with a frown,
"Good girls stay quiet, good girls sit down.
Speak less, walk slow, and don't talk to boys."
She mimicked the rules like lines in a play,
While her true self quietly faded away.

"Don't go alone, not even to the loo.
Don't laugh in public, it's unbecoming,
Don't eat too much, people are coming."
She heard "no" more than her own name,
Each boundary drawn was wrapped in shame.

"Candied Wounds: Trust Torn by Hands That Shouldn't"

One day, home alone, she sat with her colouring book.
Colouring dreams she could barely understand.
The house was quiet, the noon light soft,
She hummed to herself, her spirits aloft.

A knock, then a voice—too smooth to hear wrong,
Her uncle arrived with a smile too long.
A wolf in disguise, a demon unknown.
Called her aside, with sweets in his hand,
"Come here, little one, these sweets are pure."
She ran with delight, eyes wide with glee,
Not knowing the price of that foreign treat.

Placed her on his lap, his intentions unplanned.
His smile deceiving, his heart full of lies.
His fingers, vile, broke sacred space,
Her yellow frock stained by his disgrace.

Her cries met only her woes.

She dropped the sweets, her stomach churned,
Something felt wrong, her spirit burned.
She wriggled and pushed, her voice cracked with fear,
She cried loud, though no one could hear.
She fought with all she could muster inside,

And fled to the bathroom, where she could hide.
Locked in a world where shame and pain swirled,
A little girl shattered her trust in the world.

She sobbed as the horror clung to her skin,
She scrubbed and she cried, poured shampoo in despair,
As if bubbles could cleanse where her dignity died.
Her body ached, and she sank into a dream.

Hours passed, her mother's voice near,
A knock on the door, her mother's soft tone.
She opened the door, trembling in fear,
Ran to her mother, a hug, a sob.

The uncle departed, his smile insincere,
Waved at the child as his shame said goodbye.
Her mother, oblivious, scolded her plight,
For sleeping in the bathroom, alone for hours.

That night, in whispers, she confided her pain,
Her voice just a spark" Amma," she quivered,
"Uncle touched me here..." she pointed down
Her mother, aghast, dismissed it in vain.
"Shh..." she hushed, her panic stark,
"He's a good man; don't speak in the dark,
"They're just your thoughts," her mother replied,
Mother's breath hitched low, and hands shook wide.
"Nightmares fade," she added, eyes turned away,
Yet tears slipped down, with nothing to say.
Her mother wept but showed disbelief.

Mother pulled her close, as if time could rewind,
A fragile hush in a world unkind.
Her silence cracked in a quiet gasp—

The truth too sharp for her heart to grasp.

Her tears merged in silence, unanswered, unknown,
The weight of her truth left her utterly alone.
A wound in her trust, a festering seed.
Her heart grew quiet, her voice turned weak,
Carrying a burden no child should keep.
She closed her eyes, a restless sleep,
A childhood stolen, her soul to keep.

From then, her freedom was locked away,
No fields to roam, no friends to play.
Her dresses lengthened, her spirit confined,
A caged butterfly, her wings resigned.
Kajal forbidden, her world grew small,
Her questions unanswered, her voice met a wall.
Why was she wrong? What crime had she made?
This was her childhood—her life, betrayed.

Teenage: "From Shadows to Light"

Now she is a teenager, a spirited soul,
Carrying the weight of childhood wounds—
Unhealed, unseen, but not unforgotten.
Yet within her, teenage dreams unfurl,
Delicate blossoms amid the scars.

She found solace in art,
Her refuge in colours and lines.
Each stroke brought her fleeting peace,
Though the world around her remained colourless.

In the confines of a joint family,
Where daughters outnumbered voices of hope,
Sending a girl to school was deemed progress.
Yet the air was thick with age-old whispers,
Discrimination etched into the walls,
And daughters groomed only for domesticity.

No one taught her to dream of stars,
But within her, galaxies bloomed.
Her mother, bound by love and regret,
Became her silent advocate:
"Study, get a job, escape this village."
Her words carried a lifetime's yearning—
A hope her daughter would not share her fate.

Her father, distant, unseeing,
Never saw the beauty of her drawings,
Never offered a touch of affection,
For him, she was a burden to monitor,
A shadow to control.

As the years passed, her beauty grew—
Her form radiant, her hair a cascade to her knees.
But she never paused to admire her reflection.
Sometimes mirror betrayed her, pulling her back—
To a ten-year-old girl in a yellow frock,
Frozen in a nightmare of that monstrous uncle's bad touch.
Her body trembles, tears fall unbidden,
And she flees to the bathroom to cry,
For some traumas echo endlessly in silence.
Yet she persisted, rising with quiet resolve.

In her studies, she saw her escape,
A path to freedom paved with knowledge.
Her drawing canvas burst with vibrant hues,

A defiant contrast to the pallor of her days.

She found harmony in nature,
A soothing balm to her fractured soul.
Now, as a teenager, she stands resolute—
A dreamer with a thousand aspirations,
Her spirit unbroken, her hope alive.

Love: The Portrait of Her Heart

In a village bound by unwritten laws,
Where affection felt like a stolen cause,
She walked alone, with dreams as her guide,
Her mother's warmth her only tide.

Then came the day, her brush took flight,
In an art contest where her soul turned bright.
Her drawing, a winner—her very first prize,
And the joy lit sparks in her startled eyes.

A boy approached with a radiant face,
His smile, a melody, her heart's embrace.
He was too fair, like the morning sun,
His brightness a world she could not outrun.
"Wow, it's amazing—just like you,"
His words, a warmth that felt so true.

Her cheeks turned pink, her heart turned cold,

Yet in his gaze, a story was told.
Days turned to weeks, their smiles would meet,
In his presence, life felt sweet.

But one day, his desk sat stark and bare,
The air of the classroom, void and unfair.
Her heart ached in ways she could not explain,
Happiness in his presence, absence brought pain.
"What is this feeling?" she asked her friend,
"Why does his smile make my sorrow mend?"
Her friend, with a grin, spoke tender and slow,
"This is called love; now you know."

But love, in her world, was a whispered sin,
A forbidden dream that couldn't begin.
"Good girls don't love," her thoughts did chide,
"Am I bad?" she questioned, with tears to hide.

She avoided his gaze, ignored his plea,
Hiding her heart where none could see.
But he, with eyes so innocent and kind,
Asked softly, "Why are you avoiding me?"
His eyes searching hers intently.
With a smile that masked her silent despair,
She whispered, "There's no problem, I swear."

Then, with a glow that lit up the skies,
He asked, "Could you draw me, as a birthday gift?"
Her heart skipped a beat, her hands grew still,
To draw his face—it gave her a thrill.

For the first time, her brush found a muse,
A boy whose smile healed her inner blues.
She poured her soul into every line,
Each stroke a whisper, a love divine.
Drawing him was her quiet confession,
A meditation of pure expression.
Her wounds dissolved in the colours she chose,
The depth of her feelings in the portrait arose.

It was no mere sketch, no fleeting art,
It was her Taj Mahal, the shrine of her heart.
No canvas before, no canvas after,
Held the bliss of that joyous chapter.

For in her strokes, her spirit found flight,
Her love immortal, bathed in light.
In his portrait, she left a piece of her soul,
A tender offering, her heart made whole.
For the girl with scars now knew her part,
Healing began with the art of her heart.

On his birthday, with trembling hands,
She gave him the portrait she'd drawn with strands
Of her heart and soul, her secret art,
A gift that spoke from the depths of her heart.
His eyes sparkled, alive with delight,
"Am I this beautiful?" he teased, light.
Laughter rippled, a melody shared,
A moment where neither felt unprepared.

Art became the bridge between their souls,
Uniting them beyond what words could hold.
He leaned closer, his voice a sigh,
Whispering softly, "I love you," nearby.

Her cheeks turned crimson, a blossoming hue,
Her heart raced wild, yet her words withdrew.
She didn't reply, but her gaze confessed,
A thousand emotions her eyes expressed.

She turned and ran, laughter trailing behind,
Her joy untamed, her spirit unconfined.
The rain touched her cheeks, the earth aglow,
As nature itself let its blessings flow.

The sky wept gently, as if it knew,
First love had blossomed, tender and true.
Within the walls of a school,
A love so pure defied every rule.

Her eyes sparkled, her heart danced free,
In that fleeting moment, eternity.
For love, like her art, painted her sky,
A masterpiece she couldn't deny.

"Brushstrokes of First Love"

In the bliss of her first love,
Days drifted gently, like whispers above.
Her heart danced to a melody sweet,
Every moment with him made her life complete.

His smile, a spark, his gaze, a flame,
Each glance, each moment, never the same.
Love flowed softly, like a river serene,
A bond unspoken, tender and keen.

They spoke in letters, words so few,
Their eyes told stories the world never knew.
In silence, their love would brightly glow,
A treasure they guarded, lest others know.

She painted his face, again and again,
Each stroke a rhythm, a love's refrain.
Her canvas held their secret story,
His gentle spirit, her silent glory.

Art became their bridge, their song,
A bond that grew steadfast and strong.

Her love gave wings to her quiet resolve,
To break free from the norms and evolve.
She studied harder, her dreams in sight,
To live on her terms, to chase the light.

Their love was pure, untouched by the flesh,
A union of souls, a bond so fresh.
They dreamt of futures painted in art,
Of lives entwined, yet free in heart.
Her heart poured out in vivid shades,
His innocence glowing through tender blades.

With love, they found a sacred space,
Where passion and purity shared their grace.
Her first love, a tale of beauty untold,
A story of innocence, pure and bold.

The Silent Separation

Their love, a flame in quiet grace,
Shielded from the world, in a secret place.
But fate conspired, and one cruel day,
The shadows turned dark, love swept away.

A letter discovered, her father's wrath,
Turned their haven into a thorny path.
His voice like thunder, his eyes ablaze,
Her tender world consumed in haze.

"How dare you shame this family's pride?"
He scolded her harshly; her tears denied.
The belt struck sharp, her skin turned red,
Each blow a message her heart still read.

Her cries echoed, but mercy was none,
The love they cursed had only begun.
They left her hungry, a punishment cruel,

A lesson to teach, they played by their rule.

"Do it again, and you'll see no school,
You'll scrub the floors; don't play the fool."
Her dreams were caged, her spirit bruised,
Her love condemned, her worth abused.

They stormed to her school, their anger wild,
Demanding answers about their child.
The boy was scolded, his parents shamed,
Their love denounced, their honour claimed.

"Promise us now, you'll stay away,
No more letters, no games to play."
His parents' tears made him comply,
A heavy heart beneath the sky.

Her parents dragged her to a new school gate,
A stranger's halls to seal her fate.
Both hearts shattered, their tears untamed,
A love so innocent now harshly blamed.

He watched her leave from a distant place,
A longing etched in his tear-streaked face.
Before the end, with no one near,
He whispered softly, for her to hear:
"Wait for me, until I've grown,
When I have a job, a life of my own.
I'll find you again, no matter how far,
My love for you will guide like a star."

Her heart clung to his words so true,
A fragile hope in skies of blue.

Though torn apart, she cherished still,
A bond unbroken, a love of will.
She cried alone, her heart in pain,
Dreams drenched in sorrow, hope in vain.
For now, their paths were worlds apart,
Yet their love lived on, in each beating heart.

"Chasing Dreams, Defying Fate"

With scars etched deep in her tender heart,
She sought healing in wisdom and words, her art.
Dreams ignited, a flame burning bright,
Hope her beacon, her guiding light.

Excelled in her studies, the pride of her class,
Garnered praises that none could surpass.
Yet schooldays waned, the journey anew,
College awaited, horizons to pursue.

The family convened, a solemn decree,
An assembly where youth bows to pedigree.
In Indian homes, where tradition prevails,
The dreams of the young are chained, curtailed.

Voices of elders, firm and austere,
Shaped futures in ways stark and severe.
The patriarch spoke, his verdict stern:
"She's eighteen, love once her concern.

Marriage is due; let's set her fate,
No time to study, no room to wait."

Her heart trembled, her voice broke free,
"How can I marry? What about me?
I've earned my marks; I've yet to grow,
College awaits; my dreams must flow!
Please don't shatter the future I've earned."
Tears welled up as she begged and cried,
Her mother too, with sorrow untied.
"Let her study; she's but a child,"
The mother pleaded, soft and mild.

But the father's voice, like thunder, rang,
"We men decide!" his authority sang.
Two women wept, their pleas ignored,
Their hearts shattered, their hopes deplored.

But word of her plight reached distant ears,
Her teachers, her mentors, dispelling fears.
They came to her home, respect in their tone,
To plead her case, to make her known.
"She's brilliant," they said, "a mind so rare,
Let her study; show her you care.
With her marks, college is free,
An opportunity vast as the sea."

Their words struck chords, softened stone,
Not love but pride made the elder condone.
For to turn away guests would tarnish his name,

And so he conceded, quelling his claim.

Through prayers, tears, and collective might,
Her dreams emerged from the shadowed night.
Allowed at last to embrace her quest,
To soar, to thrive, to give her best.

From a schoolgirl bound, to a college star,
Her spirit proved wounds can't mar.
With fire in her soul, she faced the strife,
And stepped into a new chapter of life.

College days

She is a resolute spirit,
Quiet and composed,
Diligently pursuing her studies,
Her smiles, a rare treasure.
All she yearns for is freedom,
And reunion with her beloved.

In college, her circle was small,
Quality over quantity, her guiding principle.
To some, she was old-fashioned;
To others, a timeless village beauty.

Many boys sought her attention,
With professions of love,
With veils of desire,
With words laced in deception.
But her heart remained untouched,
For her prince awaited her from school.

She trusted his promise,
That he would return for her
When the time was right.
No fleeting crush could sway her,
No momentary infatuation could breach her resolve.
To her, love was sacred,
A gift found only once in a lifetime
Her dreams were clear:
To learn, to work, and to build a life with him.
Her days were steeped in books,
Her solace found in words and strokes of paint.
The only hues in her world
Were the vibrant shades
That bloomed on her canvas.

Forced marriage- chained soul

In her third year of college, she dreamed of the skies,
Her heart set on knowledge, her spirit to rise.
But one fateful evening, a proposal arrived,
A rich foreign man, with fortune to guide.

Her family, so eager, spoke of his wealth,
Astrology promised her a future of health.
"Marry him, daughter," her father implored,
But her heart was steadfast, her dreams were ignored.

She stood firm, her voice quiet yet clear,
"No, I want to study, my path is sincere."
But her words fell like whispers, unheard in the storm,
The weight of tradition began to transform.

The ceremony began, preparations were made,
But she, like a shadow, felt her spirit fade.
Her father's hand struck, his anger ablaze,
Her family's harsh words like an unholy haze.

"He's good, he's rich, you'll never find better,"
They scolded her dreams, they shattered her tether.
Her future was stolen, her voice torn apart,
Her education silenced, breaking her heart.

But in secret, her heart still held on tight,
For a love she had known in the school's fading light.
He was her prince, her hope, her belief,
A promise made, a love beyond grief.

Though the ceremony bloomed, her heart turned cold,
A future she never wanted, a story untold.
With each passing step, she felt farther away,
From the love that had once lit her way.

In silence, she stood, as the vows were exchanged,
Her thoughts with him, though her life had been changed.
With a heavy heart, she bore the weight,
As he tied the knot, sealing her fate.

A wife by force, not by her own will,
Her dreams shattered, her soul standing still.
Her eyes were teary, her spirit torn,
The colours of life were all but worn.

No love to hold, no joy to find,
Only sadness etched deep in her mind.
Her heart, once full, now hollow with grief,
A future denied, a love in brief.

First night –"Crushed body and mind"

She entered his house with a heart full of bleed,
A new life to begin, but no one to heed.
The walls were cold, the air thick with doubt,
They judged her looks, her gold, what she's about.

New faces, new voices, none kind, none warm,
They saw her as a prize, not a soul to adorn.
Her first night came with a silence so deep,
A sorrowful weight, like a wound she couldn't keep.

Her heart ached with grief, her thoughts far away,
To the love she once held, now so far astray.
She entered the room, the air heavy with dread,
The bed where she'd sleep, a place of despair instead.

He stood before her, his eyes cold as stone,
No tenderness in his gaze, no love ever shown.
As he approached, she trembled inside,

Her body no longer hers, her soul had died.

He tore at her clothes with hands that were rough,
No words of affection, just an act so tough.
She wanted to scream, to run far and wide,
But she was trapped, with nowhere to hide.

Her mind screamed in silence, her heart torn apart,
For the sacred bond was now marred from the start.
The love she had cherished, the purity she protected,
Now tainted by a man who just married her body
Her body no longer her own, but his to claim,
The first night was a storm, and she bore the blame.

Her "tali" felt like a weight on her chest,
A symbol of ownership, not of love's sweet rest.
She felt no tenderness, no warmth in his touch,
Just a void of sorrow, that hurt her so much.
As he left her there, she lay still in her pain,
Her thoughts flooded with memories, now in vain.

The night that should have been hers to embrace,
Was stolen by a man who never knew grace.
In her heart, she wept, for love she had lost,
Her dreams now shattered, no matter the cost.

Her heart once full of dreams, now hollow and still,
She saw no escape, no hope, no will.
Her voice lost in silence, her spirit laid bare,
For in this new life, no love would she share.

The Shadowed Silence

In the dim-lit room, where hope once breathed,
A young woman sat, her dreams unsheathed.
Shattered and broken by the man she wed,
Her bruised soul whispered the words unsaid.

A question she asked with trembling fear,
Her voice a whisper, yet crystal clear:
"May I continue, finish my studies?
One more year, it's not what it seems.
I'll study at home, my books in hand,
Just exams to write, then I'll help us stand
Strong for our future, and provide,
For our children, with you by my side".

But her plea was met with anger, sharp and cold,
A harsh slap that left her feeling bold.
The mark of pain spread across her cheek,
Yet her resolve stayed, though fragile and weak.

She tried once more, her tears a stream,
Her voice a thread in a desperate dream.
"Let me help, let me make us strong,
Together, my love, we'll stay alive."

But his laughter echoed like a whip's crack,
"No woman in this house will walk that track.
No man here needs a woman's coin;
Stay in your place, where you are enjoined."

With those words, he walked away,
Leaving her soul in disarray.
She crumbled down, her knees to the floor,
Her tears forming rivers, her heart a sore.

"Why, O God, must you steal my light,
And paint my skies with eternal night?
From my youth, I dreamt, I vowed,
Not to live like those who silently bowed.

Not like my mother, nor grandmother's chain,
Their silent struggles, their unshed pain.
But now I see, I wear the same shroud,
Their fate is mine," she whispered aloud.

Her thoughts wandered, carried by despair,
She slept on the floor, her spirit laid bare.
Hours passed; the night grew cold,
A new chapter in sorrow would soon unfold.

He returned, the room dark as sin,
His heavy steps where silence had been.
He called her name; she froze in place,
A trembling fear washed over her face.
"Did it hurt?" he asked, touching her cheek,
A twisted smile, his words oblique.
"I can heal it with kisses," he said with glee,
"Come to bed, my love, come to me."

Disgust filled her, but she hid it well,
Her heart trapped in a private hell.
"No, not tonight, I am weary, my dear,"
She said, her voice laced with quiet fear.

The second slap came, harder than the first,
His words like venom, his anger burst:
"You dare defy me, you lowly wretch?
It's not a request; I'll not be stretched.
I decide when, I decide how,
You're mine to take, here and now."

He dragged her close, tore at her gown,
Her dignity crushed, her spirit thrown down.
She closed her eyes, her body a stone,
Her mind retreated, she was alone.

His touch was a fire that burned her soul,
Her tears had dried; she'd lost control.
As he took what he claimed was his right,

She lay unmoving through the night.

A cadaver of flesh, with a heart that bled,
Her dreams now silent, her dreams long dead.
And yet, through the darkness, a whisper came,
A voice within, a flickering flame.
“Is this my life? Is this my fate?
Will I die in silence, consumed by hate?”

That night, in countless homes so wide,
Women faced their struggles, side by side.
Through silent tears and hidden pain,
In India, many shared the same strain.

"The Child That Never Was"

Every night, in the dim-lit room,
She curled up, waiting for sleep to come.
But before dreams could take her away,
His heavy footsteps filled the space.
She closed her eyes, her body stiff,
She knew what was coming next.
A storm of pain, a wave of fear,
His hands, his weight—nowhere to escape.
No love, no kindness, no gentle touch,
Only anger, only control.
She lived like a prisoner in her own home,
Trapped in a life she never chose.
Then one day, a tiny hope,
A life inside her began to grow.
A child, a light, a reason to fight,
A silent wish for something more.
That night, with courage, she softly spoke,
"I am carrying your child," she said.
She hoped, just once, he'd hold her close,

Or let her rest, just for the night.
But kindness was a stranger to him,
He laughed, he mocked, he turned away.
Then once again, he took what he wanted,
Ignoring the pain in her broken frame.
A sharp, deep ache tore through her soul,
She clutched her belly, something felt wrong.
A scream escaped, but no one listened,
Alone in darkness, she bled, she wept.
Morning came with flashing lights,
A hospital bed, a doctor's frown.
A quiet room, an empty womb,
Her baby gone, without a sound.
She lay there, hollow, barely alive,
Her body weak, her spirit torn.
Eyes staring at the pale white walls,
A silent prayer, a final sigh.
Would she heal? Would she rise?
Or would the world forget her cries?
No one knew, no one cared,
She lay there, alone, in her despair.

"From Pain to Power"

In the silence of the hospital bed,
Her body bruised, her spirit broken
No tears to shed, no sense of relief.
She whispered, "I've lost my child, I've lost my way,
My heart is shattered, led astray.
No love to hold, no dignity,
Why should I live this life of misery?"

Pain arrived like a thunderstorm, fierce and wild,
Ripping through her heart, leaving her soul beguiled.
A moment so dark, it was hard to breathe,
A heavy weight, like the burden of grief.

It struck without warning, uninvited, unkind,
Leaving her broken, unravelling her mind.
She questioned everything at her very core,
"Why did this happen? What is this for?"
But in the quiet depths, when the storm seemed still,
A flicker of strength began to emerge.

In her aching soul, a fire began to grow,
A force deep inside that she began to know.
A will to rise, a choice to awake,
Not the absence of fear, but the courage to break.

She stood, reborn, her heart overthrown,
A woman reformed, no longer alone.
From the depths of pain and the fight,
A decision emerged, clear and bright.

A moment of truth, a choice to be free,
To claim the power buried deep within her.
"I choose life, I choose to rise,
No longer bound by love's cruel lies.

No longer a toy, no longer a slave,
I won't be broken, I won't be depraved.
The killer of my joy, my trust,
Shall not claim my soul, nor turn it to dust."
She shed those chains and stood alone,
No longer a victim, no longer thrown.
She chose her path, despite the past pains,
Her heart may be scarred, but she'd break these chains.

With each step forward, she grew more strong,
Her spirit unyielding, where she belonged.
A decision was more than just fleeting thought,
It was the breaking of chains, the battles she'd fought.

It was the moment she said, "I will not remain,
In sorrow's grasp, or in pain's cruel reign."
It was the choice to heal, to rise above,
To take back the life that she was worthy of.
A decision wasn't just a change of mind,
It was the reshaping of a life, redefined.
Pain led her to places she'd never choose,
But in its depths, she often found the truth.

Determination rose, though battered and worn,
In its fire, a new self was reborn.
Then came the decision to break free from the past,
To embrace the future, to make it last.

In pain, she was tested, but in her decisions, she rose,
A testament to strength, beneath stormy woes.
Here she stood, with the past behind,
Determined to live, to seek and to find,
The peace she deserved, the strength she now claimed,
The decision to live, no longer the same.

She chose not to be a wife, nor wear a chain,
She chose not to return to that house of pain.
She vowed to heal, to stand alone,
To start anew, to build her own.
She chose to live for herself that day,
With courage, she set out to find her way.

Unchained

After the hospital's heavy door,
She walked once more to her own front door.
Not to cry, not to play the victim,
But to tell them all: "I choose to live."

She stepped inside, weary but bold,
Eyes burning with stories untold.
"I'm leaving him," her voice rang clear,
A truth her father refused to hear.

"Divorce?" he thundered, fists clenched tight,
"No good girl shatters vows in flight!"
She met his fury, firm, unshaken,
"A good girl breaks, but I am awakened.
I don't seek 'good,' I seek to be free,
To carve a life that belongs to me."

His hand rose high, a lesson learned,
But in the air, his wrath was burned.
Another hand had caught his strike,

A trembling voice, now fierce as firelight.
"Don't touch my daughter!" her mother stood,
A wall of strength where fear once stood.
For years she bowed, for years she bent,
Tonight, her silence came to end.
The father faltered, stunned, betrayed,
He'd never seen her so unafraid.
Yet power surged through mother's veins,
A love that cut through iron chains.
"Adjust to your husband," father coldly said,
"Forget," he warned, "or leave this place,
No daughter of mine brings such disgrace!"

She laughed—a sound both sharp and bright,
A phoenix rising into flight.
"Then let me burn, let me be gone,
I'd rather walk alone at dawn
Than drown beneath these rusted rules,
A puppet bound by ancient fools."

She turned to her mother, her gaze held pride
A whispered "thank you" from a child.
Then to the door—no chains, no ties,
Just endless roads and open skies.
And as she walked, heart fierce and free,
She knew the world would test, would see—
But she had conquered fear that night,
And stepped into her own birthright.
Behind, her mother watched her go,
A silent prayer, a burning glow.

Her Second Life

She walked away, no chains, no ties,
Under open streets, beneath open skies.
No father's house, no husband's rule,
Just quiet nights, a hostel room.

The courtroom walls had echoed loud,
Yet she stood firm, unbowed, unbowed.
A paper stamped, a battle won
No longer his, she was no one's.
No alimony, no borrowed gold,
Only freedom's fire to hold.

With weary hands, she stitched all day,
Thread and needle, scraps of pay.
But when the dusk wrapped life in grey,
She spread her colours, found her way.

Once a child with dreams so wide,

She drew love on canvas, side by side.
Now her hands, though rough with thread,
Brought lost colors back from dead.
Sketch by sketch, stroke by stroke,
She sold her art, she barely spoke.

A second-hand bulb, a tattered book,
By candle's breath, the pages shook.
Numbers, words—old friends she knew,
Calling her back, pulling her through.
By day, a tailor, by night, she learned,
For a degree was a dream unearned.

The past still whispered, the world still sneered,
Yet in the mirror, she saw it clear—
Not a daughter cast away in shame,
But a woman, rising, in her own name.

The Woman Who Painted Her Destiny

By candle's glow and pages worn,
She rebuilt the self-others torn.
She studied hard, she forged ahead,
The world once small, now vast and wide,
She walked its roads with fearless stride.

A suitcase packed, a ticket bought,
She left behind the wars once fought.
Now cities called, the ocean gleamed,
She lived the life she once had dreamed.

By day, she worked, a steady hand,
A woman strong, a life well-planned.
By night, her canvas came alive,
With colours bold and dreams revived.

The nights were long, but so divine,
Each painting grew, each curve, each line.
From humble space, a gallery grew,
Her art, her soul, so pure, so true.

Her art spoke truths she could not say,
A voice for all who'd lost their way.
Brush in hand, she painted pain,
Yet wove in hope like golden rain.

The whispers came, first soft, then loud,
Her name began to form a crowd.
From empty walls to grand displays,
Her work adorned the city's gaze.

From markets small to gallery light,
Her works adorned the walls so bright.
Critics paused, the nation took note,
Her passion poured from every stroke.

Apprentices sought to learn her art,
Inspired by how she'd made her start.
Exhibitions in cities far and near,
Her name brought hope, her craft brought cheer.

And soon, the country began to see,
A voice, a vision, wild and free.
From nameless girl to whispered fame,
They now applauded her once-shamed name.

Yet never once her family came,
No father's pride, no grandpa's shame.
But deep within, she knew so true,
Her mother smiled at all she knew.

"Meeting Her Love, One Last Time—As a Victorious Woman"

One fine day, in painted halls,
Her past returned with gentle calls.
A voice she knew from school years,
Her school love, her only love
A love once lost, but never blind.

He stood before her, warm yet changed,
With eyes still kind, though years estranged.
No longer soulmates, no fleeting past,
Just souls that met with silent eyes.

A ring now rested on his hand,
With two young children by his stand.
A family built, a love now gone,
Yet nothing felt like it was wrong.

He smiled, she laughed, the years untold,
The bitter past no longer cold.
He asked her life, she bared it all,
The rise, the fall, the battles tall.

He whispered soft, "I should have tried,
I swore to find you, yet I ignored."
She shook her head and laughed once more,
"Life played its game—there's nothing more."

"Remarry," he said, "find love anew."
She met his eyes, her soul so true.
"I have my art, my dreams, my flight,
My love's not lost, it's bathed in light."

They parted then with hearts at peace,
No chains, no weight, just sweet release.
No sorrow left, no wish undone,
Just stories told, and battles won.

Free Bird: Unbound and Undone

She walked outside, the world so bright,
The stars above in endless flight.
Once, her world was stripped of hue,
But now she lived in colours new.

With hands once bruised, she now creates,
With heart once crushed, she opens gates.
Each scar a verse, each tear a flame—
A story none could now defame.

So let world come with doubt or scorn,
She is the storm, the break of dawn.
For she has found what none could steal—
Her voice, her fire, her right to feel.

Her past was pain, her life was war,
Yet here she stood—so much more.
No longer bound, no silent cries,
She was the fire, the strength, the rise.

A hope for all, a beacon tall,
A voice that breaks the iron wall.
She proved to all what life could be,
When a woman is simply—free.

END

"I am every woman who seeks love, not security.
I am every woman who dares to live, not exist."

— Quote Inspired by the spirit of Kamala Das